Verbophobia:

A Fear of Words

Brody Hughes

BookLeaf Publishing

India | USA | UK

Made with ❤ on the BookLeaf Publishing Platform
www.bookleafpub.in
www.bookleafpub.com

Dedication

For My wife, Kris, my first, last, and only muse.

also

For my brother, Cody, now you have a title to go with the author.

and,

for my father, Scott,

If David's psalms could reach the ears of God, perhaps mine will find their way through the depths to yours.

Preface

What are you afraid of? I don't mean, afraid in a way that the eight slowly gyrating legs of haggard arachnids make your skin crawl. I'm asking about fear, true, desperate, hollow, despair. Is it mortality? Is it morality? Is it the eternal fires of damnation or the nothingness of the existential void? Do you fear the past traumas of your life? Or the anger and hatred that you have suppressed? These things don't startle us, they haunt us for ages. Eons of guilt and shame, bred in the lonely hours of twilight. The ruminations of the regretful.

I am afraid of the words I haven't said. The thoughts that have been trapped inside, begging to be freed. Their warden, the notion that I am no one worth listening to. I'm not a celebrity, an athlete, or a politician. I have no claim to fame. I'm a Marine. I'm a husband, a father, and a coach. Outside of this little town in the middle of Oklahoma, I bet there aren't many people that even care to know my name. These thoughts are my cell, but maybe they could make an exodus?

I found my way out in my closest friend, Joey Sladek. (who is the best A-driver an infantryman could ask for) He has indulged many late-night phone calls and readings of first, second, and third drafts. Joey, who is hardly a fan of poetry and is much more likely to see beauty in a pair of hanging deer antlers on his living room wall, more so than anything scribed by Whitman or Frost, has told me on several occasions that my work aroused an emotional response in him. While the critical review of a former Marine with no literary training may seem obsolete or irrelevant to a professional critic, it has been the highest form of sincere praise that I have ever received.

After one such late night call, Joey and I discussed the nature of PTSD. We both were diagnosed with combat post traumatic stress disorder after our tour of duty in Fallujah, Iraq 2006. We examined the "fight or flight" responses we shared, and compared the behaviors, actions, and thoughts we experience throughout the day. Joey holds to the idea that PTSD is centered around his anger. It's true, rage and violence are commonplace in our philosophies, but I proposed that fear was the source. It's hard for men to admit to fear, much less men who become Marines (or soldiers, sailors, and some airmen). The anger is a comforting mask for fear, but make no mistake, it's fear that drives us.

And,

That is why I have put this collection together. *Verbophobia* is a fear of words. It is the fear of their structure, syntax, and meaning. In life, we may fear jumping from a plane, but only because some words told us about the danger. We fear how people will react to what we say, how they may interpret our ideas, and what reflection our words have on our character.

The poems compiled in this book are meant to show the reader that we are all afraid of the same things in life. We fear loss, the unknown, responsibility—even love can make the bravest man quake. It is my hope that my poetry will inspire people to accept the fear they have in their lives, and to confront it. What that confrontation may look like—that is up to them. I have chosen to face my fears with a pen, a rhythm, friends by my side, and a gratitude for the life that poetry gave me the opportunity to live.

Acknowledgements

I would not be who I am without my parents. It has taken me 40 years to finally believe in myself the way they have always believed in me. Thank you both for making me into the poet that I am. You filled my life with culture and wonder. There was never a dull moment in our home. No matter the chaos around, in the most turbulent storms, the eye of our family was always filled with love. I wish thank you was enough for the life you gave to me.

This collection would not be possible without the love and support of the Little Axe Community. This small hamlet just outside of Norman Oklahoma, is settled on the land of the Absentee Shawnee Tribe. The Natives to this great piece of land are known for their rich cultural diversity and their dedication to community. The connection to historical figures such as Chief Tecumseh, has helped establish a tradition that runs deep in the blood of Little Axe. The people that live here today, both native and non-native, have a heart unlike any large city or small town I have visited. I am deeply grateful to all of the individuals that I have been able to meet and build relationships with out here on the banks of Lake Thunderbird.

I would also like to acknowledge Ariel Chart International Literary Journal for publishing my debut poem " The Sun Fell" in their April 2023 issue and Wingless Dreamers Publishing and Press for including my work in the 2024 anthology "Voices From the Trenches", without your recognition I would have surely abandoned my desire to be a known poet, thank you deeply for giving me the inspiration to continue my contributions to this incredible form of art.

Finally, I would like to thank Scott Cravens. There have been a multitude of eccentric characters that have made an appearance in my story, but none so intelligently witted, gifted with words, or blindly supportive of my inner monologue. Your writing has inspired me, your tenacity has spurred me on, and your faith has given me confidence. Where most see a broken hard hearted veteran of a rich man's war, you saw the poet. I cannot thank you enough for your faith in this collection, or for your friendship.

1. Verbophobia: Part I

Don't touch the flame, or be burned,
They had always warned.
But I stuck my hand to the blade,
In rebellious acts of war.

I have never been afraid
To sacrifice my soul.
There has never been a man or beast
That could keep me from my goal.

"Break the law and pay the fine,"
They asked I change my way.
But to the rules, I paid no mind,
And still no penance have I paid.

I have never held a fear
that I couldn't control my thought.
There is no Prince or King or God
That could break my willful heart.

It wasn't till I found a place,
A fortress home outside the maze,
That I found a fear replace
The courage of my younger days.

My body, ravaged, broke, and torn,
The pillars lost—oh, how I mourn
The demise of the little boy
Whose fear was ever stray.

With time and age passing away,
Love and hate, the trials abate.
I looked deep into the absurd,
And found my fear is one of words.

The things that I could never say,
I hid behind risk and gain.
The love I failed to receive,
The love that I brought to her knees.

All were done in despair of tone,
Of what the words would have sown.
The life that I may have missed,
If what was spoken could exist.

But never was it that I could,
Free the tongue
Trapped under the hood.
The frozen air in my lung.

He that grows in Blake's Dark Wood,

The roots that dug, deep in disturbia,
The harpies eat the source,
The forest feast, my verbophobia.

*If I were to stand, as the shepherds, in the presence of
the Angel of the Lord. I would feel fear. No words would
comfort me. The combination of phonetics, the
malleability of language, the arrangement of consonants
and vowels, the dreadful definitions of those horrific
calligraphies, they bring an anxiety into the fibers of my
muscles.*

*I am afraid of all words that carry weight. I am afraid of
the consequences of my speech. I dread the
interpretation of my text. I am afraid that I will be
misunderstood and cast out. I am afraid that I will be
seen as a charlatan or a con.*

*I am afraid that the truth, will not set me free, but will
condemn me to execution.*

2. Imposter

I was born at the Cape of Fear,
Of that I should not brag.
Was only there for two short years,
Then to the Plains where now I stand.

I learned all the ways to pick a fight,
from the parents whom I was under care.
But I learned most I know of wrong and right,
From the wisdom my Step-Father shared.

He woke us up with revellie
And filled my brain with arithmetic
After all this time it appears to me
He was what made the puzzle fit.

Yet somehow I found myself again
lost to the ills that foster
The image I framed for myself
The failing fooled Imposter.

I only ever wanted,
To be what they inspired
But the path that they lay out before me,
Left more to be admired

I spent my younger days
Punished for breaking molds
I lived the bet that no regret
Would find me when I'm old.

But under that bravado
Behind my wild eyes
I served a deeper shadow
A self that I despised.

I was small and weak and timid
Though most could never tell
I struggled with who I really was
A battle I still fail.

The wrath in me and injurious pride
Caved so hard I finally lost her
I stood alone without a guide
The man, the me, the imposter.

I am no one, no special thing
no one stands with upright posture
no reason to hear these words I speak
I fear I am an Imposter.

3. Castle Keep

Rain drops like lead,
on worn out windowpanes.
The twisted fingers of branching trees,
Sound out macabre refrains.

The night becomes alive,
Just after I find sleep.
And beyond the coats and closet racks
Sits the Castle Keep.

Its grotesque stone engravings,
against a purple sky.
toxic clouds cross the bailey.
Where the dead begin to rise.

Through its halls and cobwebbed walls,
I force my legs to creep.
lost in the dark where creatures crawl,
this prison Castle Keep.

In the grand foyer lined with silver light
There stands a hulking beast.
It turns to me with eyes of red,
fangs signal for the feast.

I try and turn to run.
My plan has just one hitch.
Through the grated garden gate,
I fall into the witch.

Her skin is warped and rotting,
With a green and yellow hue.
She grips me by my very soul,
And pulls my chest in two.

I'm staring at my beating heart,
It's shallow pace is fading.
The Hulking beast toungues the crease,
while death's anticipating.

My final breath exhales in shadow,
Joining the Dead at Castle Keep.
Then I rise with tired eyes,
for all was in my sleep.

I had to look back to find myself. The inner child that I left alone when adulthood beckoned. In that memory I found these. These are some of my earliest memories. The castle in the purple night. The toxic green clouds abreast the blackened sky. The witches peeling the skin from my tiny bones. They were only the night terrors of a child, and scarier things would haunt my reality in due time, but the dreams are just as real to me now as when I was a young boy. I remember the images as vividly as I rember the birth of my sons. I can taste the fear in the back of my throat, as easily as I can conjure the images of my own hands in my mind. I have even awoken as an older man, with the lumping spasm in chest, and pondered the physical reactions my dreams have induced. Then I think of the dreams, the nightmares, that I brought home from the war. I think of how many times I lived walking through the same events in my mind. How many times I have been devoured, how many times have I seen the horror of war, that I had thought would fade the further I traveled away from the battlefield? Dreams skew reality, and the two begin to overlap. I sometimes believe, that what happens in dreams is more real than what happens when I am awake. That is why I fear sleep, because the repetition is terrifying.

Some nightmares are not filled with tearing skin from

bone, but pulling hope from heart. I met Kris when I was just a young boy. She lived just across the street and I could sit on the rear of my Stepfather's 1965 Chevy Impala and watch her play in whatever world of pretend her innocent mind would produce. When we fell in love ,we fell forever, some days I still can't feel the ground beneath my feet when she enters the room, but back then, I was a fool. I was manipulated by the world around me, and the immature notions that plague the minds of young wild boys. I began to listen to the fears of my elders, the regrets of their own misspent adolescence, and soon I wondered if I had entered too quickly into eternity. I played a devilish card, and the house burned both the king and queen. The game would take us to opposite ends of the continent, awash in the misery of drug addiction, alcohol abuse, war, suicide and the unconditional love of two small boys. Those tragic years broke us both into pieces that managed to fit perfectly after decades of being discarded. I kiss her lips every dawn, I hold her head when she is unwell, she soothes my mind when I am at peace enough to allow, our brood has grown by two, and the little boys are older now, and will soon expand our tribe by more I expect. And yet, with all the light that God had uttered into existence showering on me at the end of the darkest tunnel I have faced to date, I still fear that I am so impossible to love, a fear that we both have shared for such a long time.

4. The Queen and The Usurper

The yellow ruffled dress aligned with brighter bows,
The auburn hair and stoic stare,
Gave the girl the fairest pose.

She was a queen
With a command just and fair.
Her kingdom was a paradise, vacant,
Free of mortal despairs.

But in her land, a war would rise,
Beset on all sides
By enemies and spies.

They had an aim to take her throne,
Destroy the hearth of her holy home.

The Queen gave in
To the enemy's demand.
Their leader was a charming man.

His honeyed words and silver song,
His longing look and tailored plan,
Promised her fealty if she took his hand.

The Queen, quaint in her ruffled dress,
Was weak for love, she confessed.
Reluctantly, she waived her saving,
As she stood in perpetual waiting,
Without the King reciprocating.

She suffered the insult
'Til she could not bear it,
Then cast her worries from the tower parapet.

Down she fell into the deep motte,
The search was vast and went without end,
But they retrieved naught
Of a Queen they failed to defend.

Her golden-gilded death mask,
With amber eyes imbued,
Was lowered down with her shroud,
But not in earthly tombs.

The King fell into darkness,
The kingdom followed suit.
The light the Queen had harkened
Gave way to gusts of gloom.

The King was on a cinder,

It burned him through and through.
The judgments that were rendered,
He tricked out of his due.

The Usurper King had never known
What it means to rule.
How could he lead by any means
That wasn't seen as cruel?

Far off, unknown to he,
Pulled from the banks of the raging stream,
The once naive and beautiful Queen
Vowed on the last ruse.

The Queen would ride a horse so hallowed,
The speed would dry out her sorrow.
She found a breath out of his shadow
And pushed a pace that none could follow,
Returning to her rule.

The years she spent in pious prison,
Believing there was only one condition
To which she must subscribe—
That of a lonely ward,
A life of love much deprived.

She shuddered now at that once-weakness

But thanked the gods for lessons she teaches.
She led an army from those banks
And started toward the castle gates.

The crows had circled 'round the gallows,
Taking bits of rotted meat between their beaks.
The Usurper King had swallowed the hate in which he
wallowed,
Where peasant bodies lay along the street.

He feasted on his loneliness,
He trained himself to hate.
His subjects fell about themselves—
The hour of siege was late.

A white horse broke the dawn
And trampled down the gate.
The King admitted he was wrong;
The Queen, with mercy, showed him grace.

"You are just a foolish man,
Tempted so quickly by pride.
And if I had a similar hand,
I'd butcher pounds from your side.

But the wounds that I have suffered,
Many by your deeds,

Are the wounds that made me who I am.
These wounds open with the blood I bleed,
The pools flowing from my hands.
These fresh scars and lacerated meat—
They were all needed for the plan
That led me back to right the dream,
To mark the lessons that made me your Queen!"

5. Labyrinth

We, as all, walk this road together
Through the desolate,
The magnificent
Fields of bloom,
Pink and white floret,
And the unyielding black thorns—
The rubies they spring from our corium.

We were to walk this life,
Tearing pleasure from pain,
Like rinds from fruit,
Being told they could be
One and the same.

The presence of evil makes a case for good;
The absence of God
Makes hard the path to light.
It gives way to darkness,
It keeps cold the night.

Huddled together, an entropy phased,
We stole the past from time's immortal keeper,
Pressed each moment into oshibana—
A kaleidoscope of dreams and desire,

Tumbling the prism,
Entangling our fresh wounds—
A mosaic of all that we wanted
But cannot be.

And yet,
We continued.
An illusionist to myself,
In awe of my own deceits,
Weaving the spells,
A hex upon me,
Of my own design.
Until the sorcerer's magic faded.

Maddened by the loss of will and spirit,
I clamored for but a single taste of the power,
And turned my sights again to you.

The predictions and synchronicity,
Mentalist summoning premonitions
Of long dead souls
Whose voices whispered your name.

I reached for your hand—
A wisp all that is ,still,
Silent and insecure,
Hopeless and hollow.

I ran down the only road I have known you to travel,
And there I found your body—
Soaked in rain and sweat, pleading with disdain.
Turned and met my eyes,
Your fear, clear as day.

The words escaped me,
I begged, "let me lead the way!"
To no avail, your heart had laid the claim.
I knew what lay beyond the shade,
What struggle we would soon undertake.

And had there been another way,
I would have found respite in shallow graves.
The seeds had been sown;
And you, would not let us away.

And so, with reluctant resolve,
We moved at glacial pace towards the unknown gates.
I could feel the change when your post gave way,
And still I saw your physical shape,
Though you were more of ghost than made.

Like the men of clay,
A terror filled inside my chest—
I've lost my heart to darkened souls

And could find no other to cover my breast.

Resisting all that I was taught,
Deeper I fell, in force to climb,
But ever failing footing to find.
The hole became the place that in infantilism I reside—
Walls caked in filth and vile,
Left the light that beckoned me,
And found there I found myself—
Lost in the shadow of the labyrinth,
Where the fear had taken hold of me.

The first girl I ever cared for, I usurped her love, and was foolishly careless with her heart. We were fatherless children. That similarity alone should have been enough for me to understand the insecurities and perceived faults that she saw inside herself. I was arrogant and conceited, I believed that this world was sent for me, and me alone to enjoy the fruit and spit the rinds as the taste pleased me. I taught her how to stand on bridges and be consumed by the fire. She taught me that not all bridges should be burned, and that there are some that cannot catch fire no matter how hot the flames. We both were, and often times are still, afraid of the cruelty and coldness that the other has channeled in defense of the attacks we wage on each other. The first attempt at loving her led to a devastating heartbreak. It became a drama that was more suitable for day time television than a boys first teenage fling. There are times that I wish I could go back and spare those children the pain they would put each other through, but so much is left undiscovered if the dirt isn't kicked up and I'm thankful for the treasure we found buried there.

Even when there is an happy ending on the horizon, the aftermath of heartbreak is a confusing time for a young man. For me it became the starting point for a lifelong struggle. I cannot say if it was chemical or catalyst, but it was not long after I began High School that I began to show symptoms of Bi-Polar disorder. It would go untreated for over two decades, and then began the "merry-go-round" of prescription drugs and therapy sessions. Meanwhile, the two sides of me began an eternal battle. One that bleeds himself to empathize with the pain of the world, and another, who sets it on fire. The pains that I put the people I love through because of my inability to understand my own mind, are inexcusable. If only I could have realized sooner how they wanted to help me, but I was afraid that I would fail them. I was afraid to navigate that labyrinth, and so I reminded lost within its endless corridors. I have escaped now, or so it seems, yet sometimes when the panic grips me, I still find myself stumbling around its dead ends and faux passages.

6. Verbophobia: Part II

Speak my heart,
Draw the Sistine Chapel.
Lips pulled apart,
Share forbidden apples.

Can they know my aim
And see behind my mask?
Can they feel the sacrifice,
The burden of my task?

I was asked to lead
Men, none more prouder.
But under my command,
My voice grew no more louder.

I set a life to unlearn,
Caught in the tangled web—
Life's lessons and secrets,
The lies that we had said.

Now learned, I have to gather
The rumble in my throat
And toss my fractured thoughts
Deep into the moat.

They never settle softly
Down in that black pit,
For there is no fountain
By which they could spit.

It burns from within,
Panicking fickle flames.
They lick at the walls inside me,
Crumbling the weary frame.

The weight of words unspoken
Lies heavy in the hand,
A bag of Charon's tokens
To enter lifeless lands.

The words that I left in limbo,
Like pieces of my soul,
Remain shrouded in their silence,
Never to be told.

If I could have set the wheels
Into reverberating motion,
I could have saved the drowning
From the torment of the ocean.

I stood in perfect stillness,

My mouth a gaping hole.
Smoke rose in monstrous columns,
Burning men like chunks of coal.

I could not enunciate
The warning to our band.
I failed to articulate,
And they fell by their own hands.

My words will be forever
Uttered in hushed symphonia,
Vibrating vocals stilled
By my crippling verbophobia.

I once handed my brother a bottle of vodka and told him that it was the cure for my unhappiness. He was an alcoholic for ten years beginning from that day. I know that he does not blame me for his mistakes in judgment, and there is no resentment in him for my part in his battle with addiction. I still feel a pang of regret and responsibility for the vices I introduced my younger brother to. He was just one of the many that followed my piper's tune over the chemical cliffs of insouciant spree. I dared them all to swallow the ills that gave me my faux immortality, and I watched the multiple fall to their substance induced enslavements.

My brother has been sober for many years now, and has made his peace with his people and his God. I am proud of him and the new life that he found after his spiritual death. I hope that his strength remains. It is a strength that I, for reasons I cannot explain, am not able to posses.

There will be others, friends and aquantaces that I am called to lead or influence. I am afraid that they will succumb to the fate of the multitude, that I will lose them in the haze of my madness. That my lose words and incorrect assumptions, will lead them into the impossible dance of my nihilism.

7. How Low Was Set The Bar

Waiting on the curbside,
Summer heat aglow,
Watching for his familiar face,
Clutching a fishing pole.

Gripping it tight,
Breathing in exhaust,
The hands on the clock
Tell me the day is lost.

Looking over my hunched little shoulder,
I thought I saw his car.
I would know it 'til I was older
How low was set the bar.

Stumbling around the kitchen tile,
Banging plastic pots and pans,
The newest legs on that child—
He does what he dreams he can.

He can say five new words;
Today he learned to say "literal."
My father's voice I hardly heard—

An act I see as criminal.

He says he loves his dad
Because I can throw a ball far.
He cannot see it's sad for me
For how low was set the bar.

Band-aids over skinned-up knees,
I met the first girl you kissed.
Uncomfortable talks—birds and bees—
All the things my father missed.

I swear it's not for us,
Me, you, and your brothers.
I hope I dot the I's,
I hope I check off all the numbers.

'Cause there is time I'm making up,
Trying to teach you to be a man.
I'll hold the next decade, a less-full cup—
I just hope you understand.

We've had our journeys now,
I got as close as I could be.
From cosplay nights and firefights,
They saw the best in me.

I promised I would carry thee
All 'round life's grand bazaar.
I'm sorry I drank away the memories
For how low was set the bar.

So much I let be wasted,
Feeling victim to a father.
The rage and anger tasted,
As flavorless as water.

If my sons could hear the words
I recite inside my brain,
They would know my love for them
Was the cure to my deepest pain.

I wish I'd held them higher up,
Among emperors, kings, czars.
But I kept them low when my demons showed
For how low was set the bar.

My sons are growing older,
The boy becomes a man.
They leave like fledglings in the sky,
And I try to understand.

It's all in the makings,
Though it leaves a lasting scar.

I didn't believe I could raise a man
For how low was set the bar.

Now Chronos begins his lullaby;
My time is not off far.
My sons, I say I tried for you—
I pray I was up to par.

And as the void opens
And I embrace the stars,
I see the loves and lives they have made—
The beauty and the righteous ways,
The gains they made in the face of shame.

I feared that I would fail them,
But stand in awe of who they are.
I'm glad they will never tell of
How low was set the bar.

8. Hymnal

When all the things that matter, are clattered, and
dismayed.
Could he still climb the ladder to the palace that you
made?
Would all still be forgiven when he meets you at the
gate?
And will you hold his hand when your father shares his
fate?
He has known you since a child yet has never seen your
face.
He has known your love and glory, but he never felt
your grace.
And now he stands beside you, a sinner, and a man,
in the face of God's good love, his judgement is at hand.

"Oh, glory oh glory I stand before the lord,
and in my final moment I'll fall upon my sword.
As Thomas doubted Jesus, I'll provoke the final word.

I'll steal the thunder from your throne. And shout with
all my might.
Of how you have abandoned us, you are shadow made of
light.
You cause us all our sickness; you cause the death to life.

You offer only punishment; you bind us to the night!
How can you forgive a man, that you have filled with
spite?
How do you condemn a man when he has lost his fight?"

And on his holy throne the Lord gazed into him
And said without a change of face "my will is at my
whim.
I am the great and perfect one infallible as my only son
The death and life and suffering is what left angels
coveting
Free will and all the righteous love, is made of all my
light
I beg of you forgiveness boy, please resume the fight!"

He stood upon his feet again, no longer bowed in prayer
And vow that when "we meet again, he will judge me
fair."
Beyond what we have made on earth, the soul is not for
sale
For if his love is from above, It can surely reach through
hell.

My Stepfather, was the man who raised me. He became my Dad, when I was ten years old. By that age I had already become an angry and rebellious child, and my Dad would and has since, suffered every attack a rebellion could muster against the state of his authority. He has employed every tactic, even falling to his knees begging for the strength to keep me, his son, on the straight and narrow path. It is the truest love I have ever known. I look at my oldest son, we have the same blood that my Dad and I share, and I know that our bond is unbreakable. I know this because of my Dad. I fear that I will never be able to repay him the debt he claims, I never owed.

9. Hiawasse

We were on the edge,
Water 30 feet below.
Eyes were locked,
Our hands were clasped,
But halfway down, we let go.

Nothing more free,
The world underneath our feet,
90's jams and Natty cans—
Bittersweet.

I never really liked that spotlight,
Ring leader, life of the party.
I just wanted to get away,
Wanted to have a life worth starting.
But I always loved you,
And for that, I'm sorry.

It's like a film
That can't roll the credits.
I've tried to kill the finale,
And I'm sorry for the edits.

When I was falling, I lost my grip,

Dangerously close to the edge of the cliff.
The shame and the guilt
I've looked to erase, standing on the ledge—
Water 30 feet below.
I promised I would hold your hand,
But halfway down, I let go.

But it all comes back around in time.
All the things we lose—
Eventually, we find them there,
The things we haven't used.

Our minds, our faith, friends and foes,
The love that we abuse—
They circle back with a second chance,
Where past and future fuse.

In an act, the claws retract,
Forgiving the obtuse.
Time turns back, discovering
That we always had the tools.

To shield ourselves from forming fears,
To harden hearts and deny a tear.

But the heart beats race
Every single time I think of home.

I look over the precipice,
To the water 30 feet below—
And I'm sorry
That I ever let go.

10. Dealer

I heard his name on the news,
The first time I had heard that name in many years.
Years since we had fished crawfish
From the red mud banks of the creek on Del Aire.
He had been a shy child,
Dirty blonde hair and sun-kissed skin,
Never one to brag or boast—
So humble,
In contrast to me.
We grew older;
I found my way to fly,
Head higher than my peers,
Carefree and fearless,
My eyes always piercing the center of the sun.
His head, ever heavy, gazed intently,
Fixed only to the ground,
Watching with angst
The solitary path he traveled.
I watched him,
Through the smoke and exposed breast.
In his expression,
I felt the infinite sadness
Behind his sodden eyes.
I sensed a desire—

A wish to live as free as I:
Free from fear and insecurity,
Free from being left alone,
Sidelined
In the game of life.
I heard his name on the news
While I ate twenty-five-dollar steak
And rubbed my wife's thigh,
Laughing at my sons.
I heard the name I hadn't heard
In many years.
I remembered,
With a twinge of sharp,
Heated, and lasting pain,
A nostalgic wound
Of younger days,
Buried deep now
In the cemetery of the forgotten past—
The days I offered him
The hops, and weed,
The snow and ice.
I remembered when
I heard his name on the news.
How quickly his curious yearnings
Gave way to freedom,
And then enslaved him.
How easily I walked away,

How I left him alone
With worry and diffidence.
I heard his name on the news.
I heard the recognizable voice of his sister,
Cracking and breaking,
Unable to repeat
That he had died,
Beaten to death in a prison cell
For the drugs he smuggled in—
A slave to the masters I sold him to.
I heard his name on the news,
And I finished my steak.

I have always felt a deep regret for introducing my friends to the vices I have indulged in. I can warp my mind into the deepest delusions, then effortlessly return to the social safety of reality. The ones that I saw succumb to their habitual need for dopamine and serotonin, I feel the weight of their shame, as if I had stolen the very self respect that had kept them from falling off the precipice of addiction and consumption. Too many of my childhood friends now sleep in coffins, victims of overdoses, suicide, and murder. I feel responsible for their failures just as much as my own. I fear that parts of my soul, have been forever lost for the sins of tempting the innocent.

The past has a sting that I find difficulty dulling out. I do not like the person I was before the war, He was weak and indesicive, unable to control situation, and worst of all, He was dishonest. I also find the man that came home from combat to be intolerable at times. There is force behind his actions, a violence and an anger that was feigned before He knew what it meant to train have hands for battle. I do not like that He abandoned his friends, but how could he face them with the blood on his hands, or the resentment he felt, and still feels towards the ones that could have sacrificed, but were too afraid to join the ranks of warriors?

I am afraid that I will always abandon them, my friends, my anchors to this life. I fear that there is an ability in me to disconnect, abruptly, from the things that have lost their value to me, even if they were precious once. I have been so careless with the treasure of friendship. I fear the specks of gold that I unceremoniously discarded on the shores of the past.

11. Little Dove

Looking down at his rosy cheeks,
His button nose, and tiny feet,
She knew then her little dove,
Oh, the things he's capable of.
She thought to herself of the things she knew.
What she could teach, what they would do?
They shared music, laughs, and food,
Tears, life, and attitudes.
He was so kind, his light shined through.
An unbroken spirit she never knew.
She thanked the stars and the god above.
Oh, what things he's capable of.
As a boy, he ran and played,
By her side, he ever stayed.
He honored his mother her hair he would braid.
And warmed her world with the smile he made.
Her peaceful son, her turtle dove,
Oh, what things he's capable of.
He lived up to her notion of a man,
Made his way with his own hand.
One morning came, he took a stand.
Shipped away to foreign lands.
He took her heart to far off sands,
A tearful stain they hadn't planned.

But he assured that he was tough,
And though the journey would be rough,
He learned to fly, little dove.
Oh, what things he's capable of.
When he returned, his days were dark,
His mother felt the fading spark.
She pressed to bridge the growing arc.
The longer stares he gained from there,
The sweat drenched sheet, the growing glare.
From fears and guilt and shame it flared
His mind alert and then he broke,
Dove spoke the words in little strokes.
As helpless as the fledgling bird
For Truer truths are seldom heard.
When words we speak, we shouldn't alter.
"Mom forgive me for the slaughter,
 What we took, in vain from them
Their sons, their mothers, and their fathers.
You raised me for peace, not violence and war,
Now days won't cease begging, what for?
I was the bird that braided your hair,
I was so pure, so kind, and fair.
Remember Mom, your little dove,
Oh, what things I was capable of."

As a wolf, the guilt of devouring the sheep, led me in search of redemption. Cody Turpen, was a sheep (only in the sense that he was incapable of true malice) in wolves clothing that brought me to the Corp. A friend that I give all the credit for my metamorphosis , before we joined the Marines, I cannot say that I was ever really living. We drank, smoked, and pillaged the values that our parents and God had instructed us to follow. It was in a moment of sober clarity that He proposed we make a mark on this world in the name of selfless altruism, instead of continuing down the road of deceit and indulgence that we had been so set on paving. We joined the United States Marine Corp.

The decision nearly killed my mother, it was 2003 and the country was at war, the thought of her baby boy joining the Marines injected her mind with images and scenarios that at one time were impossibilities, and now were the realities of mothers across the country that would send their sons overseas to defend freedom. A duty that would cost many of them their sons lives.

While, I was never my mother's "little dove", (I had to much mischief in me) I was once her only companion. We had a bond that still runs deeper than most mothers and sons, there were never many secrets between us and she knew that being reckless had long been my way. She also knew my strength was in the motivation and comfort I brought my men, and was able to help me hold it steadfast when I did begin to waiver. I am thankful for the love and support that my mother lent me during the war. I never felt her fear. The lack of that distraction kept me focused on the mission, and probably helped keep me alive.

Among our ranks however, I met many young me that were the "little doves" that shared the pure nature of their mothers. They were not the cold and hard Marines that childhood had roughly shaped into the ideal candidates for membership in this commune for Merchants of Death. They were something better, they were the Marines that stood arm in arm, weaponless, in the face of the warlords of Sierra Leone. They were noble, but they were not killers. They would have served well as the liberators we were convinced we were, but when the realization came that we were not the liberators they claimed, but we were conquers, there in Iraq, to pillage the very blood from the land.I saw them turn from meek little mice, into the ferocious demon hounds of Hell we trained to become, when rounds began to fly down range.

The bravery of the men, whom I am humble and proud

to count myself among, of the Third Battalion Fifth
Marine Regiment, has never been in question, but if
those of us that still live can face our violent past with an
understanding of the horrors we brought home with us,
still remains. I fear the meek men that unleash the
monsters inside, I fear the men that have been
consumed. I fear what our mothers think of the heartless
deeds of their "little doves."

12. We were called in

We were called in,
A convoy was hit,
 VBiED.

Vehicle
Born
Improvised
Explosive
Device

We arrived.
No KIA's.
At Least,
No friendly KIA's.

I walked around.
The sand and shrapnel scattered across the road,
Like confetti after a wedding

It was the first time I had seen,
A VBiED.

A marine picked up a piece of debris.

It was the driver's side,
Accelerator pedal.

The driver's foot had fused to it,
Only bits of bone and charred skin,
Melded with the rubber and plastic.
He held it up by the pedal.
He smiled at me.

"He had the explosives in the trunk!"

He used the bone pedal as a pointer.
He motioned like a professor,
With his macabre instrument
To the ground behind me,
As if he was Instructing me to take notice,
Of the key discussion points,
Of his lecture.

He motioned to the ground
just behind my feet.

When I turned,
I looked down,
And,

My son asks me,
To load his toy gun.
I bought it for him,
For Christmas.
He believes its from Santa clause.

He points his bony little finger
To the ground behind me.
Instructing me to turn around.

"He put the explosives in the trunk!"

When I turned,
I looked down,
And,

My wife often tells me,
That I ignore her.

I've made arguments,
In my defense.

The tv was too loud.
Or
I was on the phone.
Or
Usually its,

I was reading an article.

Tonight,
When she asked me to take out the trash.
I didn't respond.

She took after me,
In her way.
Tonight,
I made no defense.
I looked at her.
The look she sees,
When I discipline the children.
The same look
I gave her,
When I set the yard
On fire,
And I ordered her to get the hose.

She sat down on the bed.

"Why didn't you take out the garbage?
Didn't you hear me?"

I replied,

"We were called in,

QRF."
It was the first time I had seen a
VBiED.

I told her about the pedal,
And the sadistic professor.

"He put the explosives in the trunk!"

I said.

"When I turned,
I looked down,
And..."

I thought,
I did not keep trophies,
Like some other marines did.

I took one photo,
On a disposable camera,
In February of 2006.

I came home,
And took it to a one-hour photo developer.

I carried it in a book,

When technology caught up.
I scanned it into a file.
I keep it.
Hidden,
But always close.

When I turned,
I looked down,
And,

I told her,
"This is what I see,
When my sons do something sweet.
This is what I see
When the dogs need to cuddle.
This is what I see,
When I see your eyes motion to the bedroom.

It's the ever-present warning,
Of how everything I love,
Will end violently.
It's the silence before that moment,
I am shaken from a near sleep.
It's all the moments,
I'm Distant,
Or
Lost.

It's why I wince,
When I see,
How much you all love
Me.
I took this photo on the day I....
I'm always listening
For fate to catch me.
For it to take the ones I love.
It's why I can't hear you.
Because
We were called in."

*Combat PTSD feels like being a deer caught in a fence.
The panic starts, then the fight or flight, but there is no
where to go, nowhere to run, nothing to fight against. So
you fight and you run, you fight nothing and run from
nothing in every direction until you rip your hoof off to
be free, you may bleed out, but you were never really
afraid to die, just afraid of nothing. Then you wait alone
with frantic breath for the nothing to return.*

*The moments in between are filled with guilt and shame,
and a macabre sense of pride. There is guilt for surviving,
shame for the things you did you make it home, and then
there's that strange sense of justice. We tell ourselves
lies, like our cause was a more noble cause than our
enemy's, we justify our crimes with a warped morality
and pin medals on each other, then call ourselves heroes.*

*The truth that I wish I had known when I was young;
War heroes are broken men. There is no other
perspective. There is no other alternative. To do the
things a person does to become a war hero, it breaks
them. Zeimys, Johnson, Warchuck, Kelley, all of them
were heroes of the Iraq war, they all returned broken.
My father was a hero, he was broken too. I am afraid we
are all, us vets, riddled with tiny fractures. That will
eventually bring our columns down, and smite the ones*

who trust in our strength. Breaking more men in their wake.

13. In the Garden Where Nothing Grows

There are stacks of hearts,
And tiny bones,
In the garden where nothing grows.
It once held hope.
Its rows of rose,
Soil struck in bitter cold.
Withered vines left to hold,
Seeds in dust
Scattered gust.
Took our newborn son.
We laid him there,
In ground thus bare,
Dug 'til the day was done.
I'd lend my life,
At point of knife,
Too see a blooming rose.
Entangled there,
A shrine ensnared,
In the garden where nothing grows.

I have been surrounded by tragedy for as long as I can remember. I saw violence as a child, a young adult, and more as a man. Violence against man, himself, and God. I wonder, has every human soul been so prone to witness the infinite capacity for evil that we posses. Are there people that live a life where death finds them in the natural time. The first loved ones they lose are grandparents, then parents, then friends and the have the fortunate joy to part this world in the presence of their children, and not the unlivable sadness that accompanies a parent when they bury a child. I could live a thousand lives and never seen the death of an innocent child, and I would still feel the fresh pains and metal trepidation that followed the death of that dear boy. I will not write his name, and I cannot physically bring myself to recount the story of his short and needless life, I am afraid I would never recover from such a devastation.

14. He Wrote 9 Pages

He wanted to see Jesus,
To make it clear,
It wasn't her fault.
He had nine pages,
His fingers pressed like tons of rock,
Pounding down the keys,
Wearing away the years—
The shame,
The fear,
Everything he failed in trying,
The success he couldn't replicate.
His fingers fell on the keys like bombs,
Words that left his mind,
Flat as glass parking lots.
Or I assume.
He had nine pages.
He lazily scribbled
His intentions—
Flippant,
Selfish,
Pathetic in his pity.
The words merely
A predestined notion,
The act all the suicides do.

He truly didn't care.
He wanted to see Jesus,
And didn't want to blame her.
Or at least, I hope.
I don't like to think
About how he felt,
Slipping into that final sleep.
I don't read those nine pages.

When I can stop hating him, then I miss him. I'm so afraid to stop hating.

60

15. Verbophobia: Part III

A horror that was forced upon,
By fear incessant leech.
Broken into shards of heart,
When the father started speech.
Ages pass, months, and years,
Decades now beseech.
If one could simply overcome,
The tumult of its screech.
It's not until the words arise,
That flames and terror form the vice;
Grip the throats spewing lies,
Like grains along the beach.
The towers fall and my despise,
Grew until it tripled size.
I cannot face the hollow eyes,
Of he for whom I speak.
I worshipped once, I idolized,
The ground around his feet did rise.
Wearing then a thin disguise,
I swelled when he did preach.
His kingdom there up in the sky,
Fell to Earth in wild cries.
The day he swallowed pills and slurred his speech.
The father now a corpse in sight,

The sons he left aloft in flight,
We fell upon our knees and bruised our cheeks.
Though there is sweetness in the climb,
And bitterness inside.
For every holy word lay out of reach.
I pulled up on my brother,
From one bottle to another.
The hours folded in across the weeks.
We say naught to each other,
Of the trials of the Mother.
That stole a man to sweep God's golden streets.
It's the words that will divide us,
As in silence they now hide us.
From forgiveness that's a burden to the weak.
This is what we know of meaning,
The definition gleaning.
The truth that takes us to a mountain's peak.
But in this verbophobia,
This empty cornucopia,
I fear the words we never dared to speak.

A boy that lived down the street from me committed suicide when I was in elementary school. He was much older than me and my friends and none of us knew him, but I remember watching the children that had been his classmates. They were all so somber, but without any basis of understanding. They were confused and answers from adults did not give justified logic to the rumored act of self deletion. In those days suicides were "accidents" and they were hidden away and never spoken of, more words that cause us to embrace the chill of despair.

A few years later, a close family friend would lose family to suicide. When my friend was pressed on the nature of the passing, he attributed the death to a heart attack. He knew that I knew the truth and when he would give his false statements to the morbidly curious liaisons, He would look at me and say, "It's easier for me, to think the death was natural, I am afraid it would hurt to bad, if I had to think about the pain." I understand that, I am afraid I understand that.

March 2, 2008, my father, Scott Hughes, died by suicide. The chasm that his death caused, has divided my family for many years, My brother and I seldom speak about our father. I don't visit my grandmother anymore. My Uncles, Aunts, and cousins are little more than strangers.

There are so many unanswered questions, and so many forgotten memories. I think all of us are afraid the words we have been holding back.

16. When Cain Loved Abel

They say that we are speeding to a devastating end
Preachers pilfer purses and buy Mercedes Benz

The crime rates always rising downtown just ain't the
same
But hustlers always run new rackets you never change
the game

The truth is not empirical morals seldom stable
But I'll bet my back that it's a fact we were good when
Cain loved Abel.

Abortion rates are high and weapon sales are higher
But draw a line to suicide and Johnny labels you a liar

Sex is sold in schools and with our tv dinners
Donate 10 bucks to a slimy fuck and you're voting in a
winner

The cancers all the same from farm to kitchen table
But check this out I'll tell you now we were good when
Cain loved Abel.

Run and punch a ticket democracy's at stake

So billionaires and fucking squares leave scraps on our
kids plates.

Entertains bitching signaling their virtue
But they were never face to face with any of the issues

Maybe things are worse, but curse is still a fable
Man's the beast that fucked this feast, we were good
when Cain loved Abel.

After I returned home from Iraq, I carried with me an understanding of what the elite had done to the plebeians like me. They had manipulated us into killing each other, and they had been doing since the first man took another's life, for material. We are still killing each other, for money, resources, or for crossing imaginary lines. We kill in the name of God, country, and brotherhood. All of these are ideals that should be sacrificed for by showing humility and compassion, instead of shock and awe. I fear that we are too far gone to spare humanity from the ills of its own nature.

17. A Drink With Breakfast

The human race
Knows its place,
Can't fight against
Its nature.
To save its face
From great disgrace,
It creates itself
A savior.
But knowing less,
They fail the test,
And live to love
The danger.
The human race,
In all its grace,
Knows itself
To be a stranger.

18. Laying Bricks

Not a Mason,
But laying bricks.
Broken foundation,
Buildings crumble.
Ignorant hands.
Try to rebuild.
Failed renovation.
Tirelessly tinkered upon.
The bones won't last.
The steel oxidizes.
Weather, decays.
The wood will soon rot.
The paint, the first to fade.
Without Skill, repeat.
The process, mixed more
Lime and silica, still no cure.
Blueprints once held plans
A diagram, a dream.
Scribbled over,
Redrawn and illegible.
Rolled and frayed.
With flawed aim
Wrecking balls sweep debris.
Begin again.

No architect,
No engineer.
Not a Mason.
But laying bricks.

A preacher gave a sermon on the "Sin of Compromise", that I was audience to when I was a young man. He warned against allowing minor offenses against God grow into major immoral habits. He spoke on why the followers of Christ had to take a stand against the tide of temptation that was infected our nation.

It's been over twenty years and if that man of God is still witnessing to the faithless, I am sure he is crying out the warnings of compromise to this day, or at least I hope he has not compromised in his message.It has been twenty years since I gave my attentions to the lessons of God's messenger and I fear believers of every faith and dogma are still compromising belief in order to retain a lifestyle.

In truth, I think all belief is compromise. We as human beings have to compromise our, logic, rationale, even or mortality to reconcile reality with belief. It is a delicate act to be aware, to have faith and intellect, to be compassionate and yet, justified. I am afraid that it is a dance with no end. I am afraid that I will have to compromise myself, that I will be trapped in the cycle of faith versus logic, and in that eternal wheel, I will be lost.

People are afraid to not know. They fear the inadequacies of skill and knowledge that they lack when compared to others. Some are so afraid of it they feign the knowledge

*and set to a task equipped with ignorance and pride
alone. How many times I have attempted to build a life
without the knowledge of how a good life was to be
constructed? Even now the walls of my home, the
foundation that I love on feels sturdy, but I am always
afraid that my skill as a craftsman, is not good enough to
sustain it.*

19. The Gospel of a Hallowed Hate

The veins throbbed,
In their shape.
Electric and unstable.

The first taste,
Despair creates,
A damnable fable.

This dogma built on raw disdain,
The armor from oppressive pain.

Emerging From the jaws of fate,
The Gospel of a Hallowed Hate.

A verifiable truth, incapable of deceit.
Lends itself insight, to ones that couldn't see.

That find the light, inside the night,
A sacrilege belief.

As it relates and plainly states,
The Gospel of a Hallowed Hate.

A hardened heart if truly aimed,
Becomes a heart that's truly saved.

The virtue better to have lost?
That True lovers languish!
But to those that know the cost,
A most offensive language.

Navigate the dire straights,
With violence, equate!
Actions now can vindicate!
The Gospel of a Hallowed Hate.

Some say they carry burden,
That forgiveness is the way.
The integrity of its intent,
Gathered deep within the pate.

Those some will cease their anger,
Leave it at God's gate.
Knowing they were all the long,
To weak to carry the weight!

Only those with pride and wrath,
With a thirst, insatiate,
Full of rage and on the path

The unbroken demonstrate!

The beauty awe and power, Of
A Gospel of a Hallowed Hate.

20. Father Time

Father Time stands laughing,
At grains of sand in passing,
For joyous hours make a journey fly.
The angels, in their yearning,
Looked to God for learning—
All knowing fruits sprang upon the vine.
The eons waned and waxing,
The stars in glancing, dancing,
Settled on the night that you met I.
A flame eternal burning,
Beauty and pain both turning,
By fire spreading wild, younger lives.
Fate's draw became unmade,
When we spun in retrograde,
Away against the currents tossed in time.
Just as orbits travel back,
We flowed in lovers' tracts,
To a family most familiar and divine.
Inside it we found strength,
Yet in moments still am weak—
A blessing and a curse born of my mind.
You pull us like an ocean,
Divide me into quotients,
A trail beset to forever twist and wind.

But as Father Time stands laughing,
At every grain of sand that's passing,
I thank the glass for grains that you were mine.
For every mortal sin,
Each battle we are in,
I ask you, turn the dial to the sky.
Reset the broken clock,
Leave behind the lot,
And pour the sand that gives my heart to thine.

Love is the most sought after resource on the planet. It is found here on Earth in abundance. It's easier to access than water or food, and yet it is so easily lost, misused, or wasted. That is one of the most dreadful possibilities that I fear. Is there anything more terrifying than watching the person you love, drift away and fall into indifference, or casual familiarity, then they become a stranger that sees through you, instead of being the entity that once saw into you. When once loving states become Medusa's gaze, and all you can feel is cold porous stone in your heart. I fear losing love more than I fear losing my life. I fear that I will not be able to preserve precious things, because I can still remember the shiny golden things that my touch has tarnished.

I played carelessly with the love of my life; I lost her once. After the inevitable loss of so many of the brothers that I served with, I have vowed to endure. Love should be worth any hell that we pretend to suffer through. Sacrifice and selfless love for the person you love should not raise fears in the hearts and minds of the hopelessly romantic, but there is a reason they say that we "fall" into love. It is because there is nothing more frightening than clinging to the hope that our love will be returned.

21. Verbophobia: Part IV

Afraid of the answer,
 as well as the question.

Afraid that I am no one,
 that we are all the same.

Afraid of demons,
 and repetitious sleep.

Afraid I cannot be so loved,
 afraid that I am weak.

Afraid of the bridges, and the flames on the pyre,
 afraid of the fall, and the truth of the liar.

Afraid of the sin,
 of the monster that I am.

Afraid of the things that I am capable of,
 and incapable of.

Afraid of the reminiscing,
 afraid of nostalgia,
 afraid of the drinking that's done by the gallon.

Afraid of our very nature,
 of what we fail to see.

Afraid of what life is like
 if the dead would not be.

Afraid of every word
 they spoke on innocent wounds.

Afraid of living in make-believe,
 afraid of being a fool.

Afraid of understanding why
 it's easier to live the lie.

Afraid of the love that leaves me alone,
 afraid of this fictitious dystopia.

But of all these, I fear the most:
 the silent speech of verbophobia.

When you live your life afraid, everything is affected. It takes your energy, creativity, and your confidence. As the fear builds, the fearful collapse. The pressure wears the frame, and the frightened vessel sinks deeper. The only options are to cower and die, or to face the fear and fight to live.

The problem isn't knowing what your options are, the problem is making yourself act. Fear clouds our judgment, it cripples us, it forces us to have to claw and fight our way back to a state of rationale thought. The first step is to admit our fear to ourselves, to name it, to begin to learn or unlearn, how to control it.

I have feared these words for too long. I have spent a lifetime trying to make sense of the things I have done in the name of self preservation. I have played the part of the fearless man, and all along I was hiding inside my self the truth. The truth that I was afraid to really live my life. I shied away from the challenge because I was overcome with the fear that I would fail. I have wailed at the face in the mirror, tormented and haunted by the possibility that the man in the reflection was not up to the task of fatherhood, friendship, marriage, mentorship, or self love. I placated my own destructive tendencies to avoid my personal responsibility to my wife, my children, my family, and even myself. I wore the mask, out of a stark and palpable fear, that I would fail, or worse, I would succeed.

Success would have brought me into the center stage, a place where failure is an even sharper sword to fall on. It wasn't until I saw that all the tiny wounds from years of cutting myself short was already bleeding me, that I decided that I needed to face the one fear that I had hidden with the skeletons and boogeymen from my childhood, deep into the back of the closet inside my mind. My verbophobia. The only way to wrestle any courage that I might still have, was to pour these words out. For the first time since the ignorance of youth shielded me from the horror of adulthood, I am displaying my voice for anyone who chooses to hear. In the mist of rejections and consolations, I have found that I am not afraid of failing anymore. I am not afraid of my morbid thoughts, or my heresy. I am only afraid, that I can no longer be silent.

I hope that you can find a way to face your fears. That

you will rid yourself of the ghost and demons that plague your dreams, or risk becoming one. But don't trouble yourself, if you find that your hair is raising up on end, your mouth drys out pooling with saliva, the beat of your heart begins to race wildly, and you let out an uncontrollable scream, it's only fear that you face. And if you fail to confront it this time, I'm sure it will haunt you again.

www.ingramcontent.com/pod-product-compliance
Lightning Source LLC
Chambersburg PA
CBHW061700130726
47996CB00006B/2100